SCANDINAVIAN | AMERICAN
ROOTS | LIVES

Scandinavian Emigration to North America

SCANDINAVIAN ROOTS | AMERICAN LIVES

Scandinavian Emigration to North America

Nordic cooperation takes place among the countries of Denmark, Finland, Iceland, Norway and Sweden, as well as the autonomous territories of the Faroe Islands, Greenland and Åland.

The Nordic Council
is the body which embraces the parliamentary co-operation between the Nordic countries. The Council consists of 87 parliamentarians from the Nordic countries. The Nordic Council takes policy initiatives and monitors Nordic cooperation. Founded in 1952.

The Nordic Council of Ministers
is a forum for cooperation between the Nordic governments. The Nordic Council of Ministers implements Nordic cooperation. The Prime Ministers have the overall responsibility. The activities are coordinated by the Nordic ministers for cooperation, The Nordic Comittee for Cooperation and portfolio ministers. Founded in 1971.

Address:
Store Strandstraede 18, DK – 1255 Copenhagen K, Denmark

Internet:
www.norden.org

@ Nordic Council of Ministers and the author – 2000 Copenhagen
All rights reserved

Editorial committee and catalogue coordination: Krister Björklund, Marianne Möller, Birgitta Schreiber

Project Group for the Nordic exhibition on emigration:

Henning Bender, director, Danish Emigration Archives, Aalborg, Denmark
Olavi Koivukangas, director, Institute of Migration, Turku, Finland
Gisli Sigurdsson, director, Arni Magnusson Institute, Reykjavik, Iceland
Knut Djupedal, director, Norwegian Emigrant Museum, Ottestad, Norway
Dag Blanck, director, Center for Multiethnic Research, Uppsala, Sweden

Cover: Ellis Island, New York, 1895

Catalogue printed and bound by Berlings Skogs AB, Trelleborg, Sweden, 2000

ISBN 92-893-0425-1

Catalogue published with support from Scandinavian Seminar College

The steamer Urania *leaving Finland with 509 emigrants on board in the spring of 1893. Photo Captain J. A. Rosqvist.*
© F.Å.A. (Finland Steamship Company).

Overseas Migration from the Nordic Countries 1900–1904

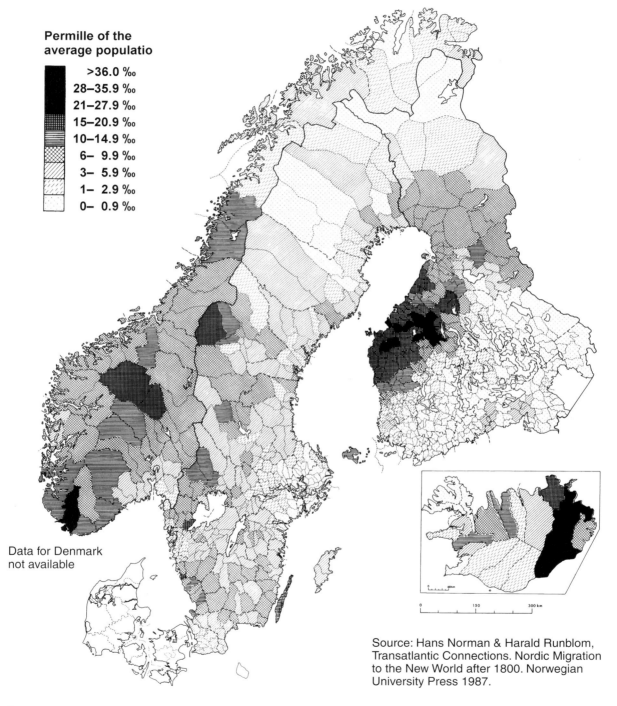

Permille of the average populatio

- >36.0 ‰
- 28–35.9 ‰
- 21–27.9 ‰
- 15–20.9 ‰
- 10–14.9 ‰
- 6– 9.9 ‰
- 3– 5.9 ‰
- 1– 2.9 ‰
- 0– 0.9 ‰

Data for Denmark
not available

Source: Hans Norman & Harald Runblom,
Transatlantic Connections. Nordic Migration
to the New World after 1800. Norwegian
University Press 1987.

The Number of Persons Born in the Nordic Countries in U.S. Census 1930 and Census Canada 1931

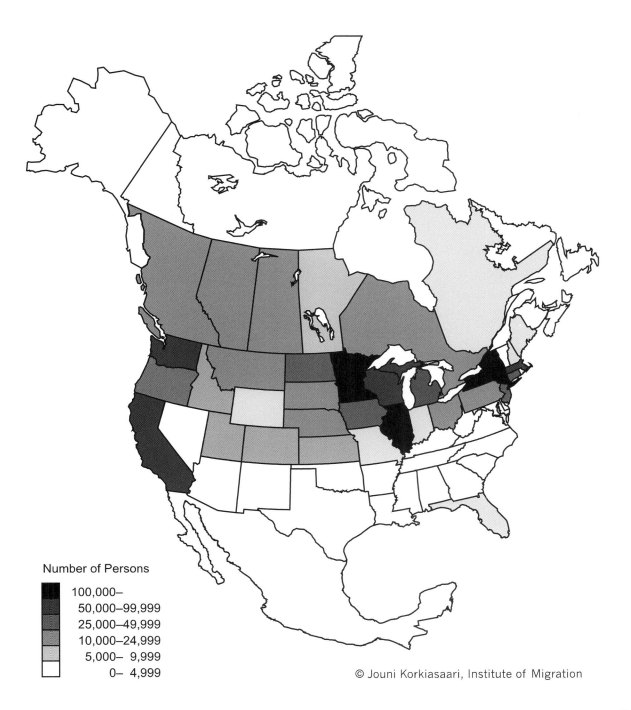

Number of Persons

- 100,000–
- 50,000–99,999
- 25,000–49,999
- 10,000–24,999
- 5,000– 9,999
- 0– 4,999

© Jouni Korkiasaari, Institute of Migration

The ticket office at Ellis Island around 1900. Note the text in Norwegian at upper left hand corner.
Photo Lewis Wickers Hine. © State Historical Society of Wisconsin.

Introduction

The Nordic peoples have a long background of migration. According to tradition, their ancestors originally arrived in Scandinavia from somewhere in the vicinity of the Black Sea. Tradition also holds that many of the Germanic tribes that overran the Roman Empire in the West during the fifth and sixth centuries A.D., such as the Goths and the Vandals, came from Scandinavia. During the Viking Age, between the eighth and eleventh centuries, Scandinavians mainly from Denmark and Norway conquered and settled large parts of the British Isles, as well as Normandy in France. Swedes moved across the Baltic and along the Russian rivers as far as the Black and Caspian Seas, establishing the first Russian state at Novgorod around 860.

Of particular interest for what would follow, seafarers from western Norway had already before the end of the eighth century settled on the Orkney, Shetland, and Faroe Islands in the North Atlantic. By round 874 they had discovered and began settling on Iceland. In 986 a Norse colony was established on Greenland that would survive down to the fifteenth century. In the year 1000 Leif Ericson and his crew from Greenland were the first Europeans to set foot in the New World. Leif wintered in a place he called Vinland. Shortly thereafter, Norsemen from Greenland attempted briefly to settle there, but were driven off by the native "skraelings." Archaeological evidence at Anse aux Meadows in Newfoundland has in recent years provided material proof of their presence in North America, although the dedicated efforts of amateur enthusiasts to demonstrate a long continued Viking connection remain speculative at best.

When Europeans returned some five hundred years later, Sweden was among the early colonizing powers in North America. In 1638, it established its New Sweden colony along the lower Delaware River, in parts of present-day Delaware, Pennsylvania, and New Jersey. The colony remained under the Swedish flag for only seventeen years, until the Dutch conquered it in 1655, followed in 1664 by the English, but a few hundred Swedes and Finns—Finland then being a part of the Swedish realm—settled there. The Swedish language and Lutheran congregations, served by pastors from Sweden, survived in the region down to the later eighteenth century. Many of the colonists' descendants followed the Frontier westward and it has been shown that their native skills became important parts of the pioneering way of life in the woodlands. Surnames traceable to New Sweden colonists are presently to be found throughout the United States.

A few Scandinavians continued to arrive in America throughout the Colonial and Early National periods. There were Norwegian seamen in Dutch New Amsterdam (later New York) in the seventeenth century and Danish Moravian Brethren in North Carolina in the eighteenth. The great migration of Scandinavians to North America took place, however, during the nineteenth and early twentieth centuries. Between 1825 and 1925, some 1,250,000 Swedes, 850,000 Norwegians, 360,000 Danes, 390,000 Finns, and 14,000 Icelanders came to the United States, while perhaps one-tenth of that total number migrated to Canada. In proportion to their populations, emigration from the Nordic countries was among the heaviest in Europe. Norway was surpassed in that respect only by Ireland. There was meanwhile an ebb and flow of Scandinavians between the United States and Canada. Of the Nordic immigrants approximately one-third eventually returned permanently to their home countries, which would be close to the European average.

The most important motives for emigration from the Nordic countries were unquestionably economic, above all rapid increases in rural populations with limited amounts of cultivatable land before industrialization could provide alternative employment. America seemed to offer boundless opportunities, not least for land-hungry farmers. But other factors also played their part: dissatisfaction with the authoritarian Lutheran state churches, especially during the earlier period; resentments created by rigidly class-bound societies; lack of political rights for the broader masses; family conflicts; even sheer lust for adventure. Each emigrant had a particular mixture of motives for arriving at the great decision.

In 1825 a group of fifty-two persons in Stavanger, Norway, purchased a small sloop, *Restaurationen*, and sailed with it to New York, thereby marking the beginning of the great Nordic migration. The "Sloopers"—like most of the early Scandinavian rural emigrants—were not poor; they had to have assets to afford the journey. In large part they were motivated by religious discontents. The group settled near Rochester, New York, but by the mid-1830s most left for the northern Illinois prairie. Their enthusiastic letters about their new settlement began attracting growing numbers of Norwegian emigrants from 1836 on. Many Norwegians soon moved on, from Illinois to Wisconsin, then to Minnesota, and eventually out to the Dakotas and the Pacific Northwest.

Although there were some early forerunners in Wisconsin from 1838 on, Swedish emigration got properly underway in 1845 with the departure from Kisa of a group of twenty-one peasants led by Peter Cassel, who established their New Sweden colony in southeastern Iowa. After them came already the next year over a thousand followers of the self-proclaimed prophet Eric Janson, mainly from north-central Sweden, who established their religious utopian colony of Bishop Hill in nearby northwestern Illinois. Letters from the Cassel and Bishop Hill colonies encouraged a sizable emigration from Sweden to the American Midwest. Swedish Lutherans soon settled near Bishop Hill and from the original cradle of settlement in Illinois and Iowa, Swedes would fan out, mainly to Minnesota, Wisconsin, Nebraska, and Kansas, later to the Rocky Mountain states and the Pacific coast. Meanwhile small Swedish and Norwegian settlements appeared in Texas.

Emigration slowed during the Civil War years, 1861-65, but Scandinavians in America served in high proportion to their numbers in the Union forces, and while some even immigrated to join and receive enlistment bonuses. Predominantly Norwegian- and Swedish-American units from Minnesota and Illinois won their share of glory in the war, showing their dedication to their new homeland.

The end of the war brought unusually favorable conditions for European immigration. The contrast between booming post-war prosperity in America and economic stagnation at home became increasingly evident. The American Homestead Law was passed in 1862, allowing any U. S. citizen or person declaring the intent to become one to acquire 160 acres of free government land. Shipping lines converted from sail to steam in the Atlantic passenger traffic while railroad construction in Europe and particularly in the vast American interior strikingly improved the price, comfort, and convenience of travel by land and sea. The American railroads meanwhile received large government land grants, which they sold off on favorable terms to settlers in their areas. Growing numbers of Scandinavians in America meanwhile drew ever larger numbers of their countrymen to join them. The mass movement, especially from Sweden, was set off by serious crop failures between 1867 and 1869. From that time on, down to the mid-1890s, Swedish and Norwegian emigration reached its peak figures.

It was after the Civil War, that large-scale emigration from Denmark, Finland, and Iceland began. There had been some early forerunners. Already in the 1850s small numbers of Danish and even some Icelandic Mormons had made their way out to the new Zion in Utah. A few Finns, mainly from Finland's Swedish-speaking coastal districts, had joined early Swedish settlements. Larger numbers of Danes would follow by the 1860s, including many from Slesvig after that province was conquered by Prussia in 1864. The Danes established fewer and less compact colonies than did the Norwegians or Swedes, but many settled in Wisconsin, Iowa, and Nebraska, and later on the West Coast. Finnish immigration peaked between 1900 and

1914—later than the other Nordic groups—and was heavily concentrated in the northern parts of Michigan, Wisconsin, and Minnesota, as well as in northwestern Oregon. Unlike the other Nordic groups in North America, most of the Icelanders settled in Canada, mainly in Manitoba from the 1870s on. From there smaller numbers moved across the border, especially into North Dakota.

By the 1880s, the patterns both of emigration from the homelands and of settlement and occupations in America were beginning to change. Emigrants from the poorer classes, both rural and urban, arrived in increasing numbers, thanks both to lower travel costs and especially to money or prepaid tickets sent over by relatives or friends already in America, which they could later repay with their American earnings. These later immigrants had fewer means to establish themselves as farmers as those who had come earlier, at the same time that less and less good Homestead and railroad land was available. Relatively early Chicago and Minneapolis had became the leading Swedish- and Norwegian-American urban centers. Now increasing numbers of new arrivals found industrial employment in mining, logging, and manufacturing, while young Scandinavian women were much in demand as domestic servants. Increasing numbers settled in cities and industrial communities, now also in the northeastern states, like the Swedes in Worcester and the Finns in Fitchburg, Massachusetts. Modernization in the homeland economies periodically created unemployment and hardship, causing new waves of emigration, like the shift to steam navigation that resulted in a large emigration of seamen and ship-builders with their families from southernmost Norway to Brooklyn, New York, beginning in the 1880s.

While the Norwegians and Swedes have remained among the most rural and agricultural of American immigrant groups, by 1910 over half of them were already urban dwellers. The Finns, arriving late, were from the start mainly in industrial occupations, particularly mining. There was meanwhile greater movement on the whole between urban and rural areas among the Scandinavians than among most other immigrant groups in America. While many Nordic immigrants and their children eventually moved to town, others worked at first in urban occupations until they could earn the means to acquire farms of their own. Many former Finnish miners, for instance, in time became small farmers in the cut-over forest lands of Michigan.

World War I, between 1914 and 1918, drastically reduced European, including Nordic, immigration. There was a brief upsurge in 1923, just prior to the passage of the first regular immigration quota law by the American congress the following year. Even smaller national quotas were set in 1927. Yet even the small quotas assigned to the Nordic countries were seldom filled after 1924, which above all reflected the rising prosperity in the homelands that made emigration a less attractive option. During the Great Depression of the 1930s, far more Scandinavians remigrated back to their homelands than emigrated to America. World War II, from 1939 to 1945, brought Nordic immigration practically to a standstill.

Since 1945 small numbers of Scandinavians have continued to come to America, although mainly of different types than their predecessors. Most of these newer arrivals have been well-educated and highly skilled professional and business people and have settled in the larger cities, especially on the coasts. Many have had little to do with the older immigrants and their descendants. They have usually retained their original citizenship and eventually a high proportion of them return home.

Nordic settlement in North America involved from the beginning not only direct immigration from Scandinavia but in large degree the stage migration of immigrants from the older colonies who moved on—usually westward or northward—to establish new settlements together with relatives and friends from home. In this way, widespread communities originating in particular parishes in Scandinavia could hold together, despite the distances between them, rather disappearing into the general American population. This process played an important part in the preservation of immigrant cultures that with time were neither entirely Nordic nor American, but a combination of both.

Adaptation to American life was on the whole relatively easy for Scandinavians. As Protestant northern Europeans they were much more hospitably received by the older Americans than were the growing numbers of immigrants from southern and eastern Europe from the 1880s on. They came from largely similar cultures and—except for the Finns—they spoke languages closely related to English, which was relatively easy for them to learn. Nordic immigrants were proud of their new identity as Americans and tended to identify more closely with the Anglo-Saxon element than with the newer immigrant nationalities.

Still, they created a vital ethnic cultural life of their own, which flourished as increasing numbers of their countrymen arrived in America following the Civil War. The first immigrant institutions were their churches, which usually appeared soon after settlement. The congregations organized into national Lutheran synods; among the Norwegians into several based on doctrinal differences. Especially during the earlier period many, especially Swedes, became Methodists or Baptists, forming their own national conventions within the American denominations. Some were Mormons, and others became Episcopalians, Adventists, or joined the

Salvation Army. A new purely Swedish-American denomination was created in 1884 when the Evangelical Mission Covenant broke away from the Swedish Augustana Lutheran Synod.

The churches long held to their native languages, establishing their own summer schools to teach it to the immigrants' children. They founded colleges, usually with seminaries, like Augustana, Luther, St. Olaf, Gustavus Adolphus, North Park, Augsburg, Grand View, Dana, Suomi, and others, originally train clergy for the various synods and denominations, which became—and remain—centers for Scandinavian cultural in America. In time several state universities established Scandinavian departments, which have cultivated an interest in the Nordic lands and their cultures outside the Nordic-American communities themselves.

Nordic immigrants were already from the beginning highly literate and both the church bodies and private publishers brought out a remarkable number of newspapers and other periodicals in their native languages, which served both to keep alive their old cultural traditions and to help them adjust to life in America. The publishing houses also printed books in large numbers, most often devotional works, practical handbooks, popular literature from the homelands, or translations from English, but also including poetry and fiction by immigrant authors about the immigrant experience in America. By far the best known of the immigrant writers was the Norwegian American Ole Rølvaag, whose *Giants in the Earth*, which first appeared in English in 1927, became a best-seller on the American book market, and remains an enduring classic.

Meanwhile Nordic immigrants established a wide variety of secular clubs, societies, and fraternal lodges. By the end of the nineteenth century, many of the local lodges joined together to form regional or national organizations, like the Danish Brotherhood, established in 1872, or Swedish Vasa Order of America or the Sons of Norway, both founded in 1896. At the same time, numerous local provincial societies cultivates the traditions of particular home regions in the native lands. There were innumerable temperance lodges, sports clubs, singing and theatrical societies, women's groups, children's clubs, and study circles. Rather apart from the Nordic-American mainstream were the growing numbers of immigrants, especially after 1900, who became active in the labor and socialist movements in America, and who had their own network of clubs, cooperatives, and publications, especially among the Finns in the Upper Midwest.

The drastic decrease in immigration by the 1920s inevitably led to a decline in the old immigrant cultural life, a process hastened by the heavy return migration during the Depression and virtual end to immigration during World War II. As a mat-

ter of survival the churches, often reluctantly, went over to English-language ser-
vices. Most of the older immigrant organizations and publications quietly suc-
cumbed, often after valiant efforts to survive. Yet already by around 1930, new
institutions had begun to appear, like the Vesterheim Norwegian-American Museum in Decorah, Iowa, the American-Swedish Historical Museum in Philadelphia,
or the American-Swedish Institute in Minneapolis, oriented toward younger, Eng-
lish-speaking Scandinavian descendants.

During the Depression, World War II, and earlier post-war decades, ethnic senti-
ment reached a low level in America. From the 1970s on, however, there has been
a strong revival of ethnic engagement among all elements in American society,
not least among the Nordic descendants. Genealogy, the search for cultural and
family roots in the old homelands, travel, and the media have established ever
closer ties between them and the lands of their ancestors. Numerous new organizations devoted to such contacts have appeared in recent years. As time has
passed there has likewise emerged the growing sense of a wider Scandinavian-
American community based on shared traditions and values.

Nordic immigrants began at an early stage to cultivate the own history of their
own groups in America, first by writing their reminiscences from pioneer days,
then collecting documents and writing historical accounts which have become
increasingly objective and scholarly down to the present. There are historical
societies in the United States for the Norwegian, Swedish, and Danish Americans, with their own archives and publications. Interest in the emigration history
meanwhile came late to the homelands. The emigrant novels of by the Swedish
author Vilhelm Moberg, which appeared between 1949 and 1959 and became
international best-sellers, aroused widespread popular enthusiasm. During 1960s
serious study of the subject at last begin at Scandinavian universities. Since then
Nordic emigration researchers have set high international standards in their field.
(For historical societies and archives, see "Sources.")

Scandinavians and their descendants have done well for themselves in America
and many have achieved positions of prominence in different walks of life. The
proportion of emigrants to the total populations of the homelands was nonethe-
less always far greater than the numbers of Scandinavians in America. The overall impact of the great migration has thus been even greater in the Nordic lands
than in the New World.

From the beginning, emigration aroused widespread alarm among conservative
circles in Scandinavia, which feared the loss of labor and military manpower, as
well, frequently, as American ideas that seemed threatening to traditional society

and culture. This resulted in much emotional anti-emigration propaganda. In Sweden and Norway after 1900 societies were established to combat emigration, although to little avail.

To Scandinavian liberals and radicals, America provided inspiration for long-overdue reforms. The emigrants themselves meanwhile wrote innumerable "America letters" to relatives and friends at home, not only encouraging others to emigrate but also arousing awareness of what would be needed to create a "new America" in the homelands. Successful emigrants often revisited their old homes and boasted of America's advantages. Many emigrants eventually returned home permanently, bringing with them new attitudes, and frequently capital and fresh ideas. Powerful American influences are evident to this day in all areas of life in the Nordic countries: in the democratizing of government and society; in science, technology, and the economy; in popular culture; above all in a markedly progressive and innovative view of life. The Great Migration was one of the greatest historical forces—if not the greatest—in the creation of modern Scandinavia.

Over the past half century the situation has been reversed as the flow of migration has been reversed, with far more immigration *to* than emigration *from* the Nordic lands. During World War II, Sweden, which managed to remain neutral, took in large numbers of foreign refugees, many of whom remained. They were followed during the post-war decades by an influx of foreign labor into Scandinavia to meet industrial needs. During the 1980s and 1990s large numbers of refugees from troubled areas of the world have received asylum in the Nordic countries, including many from outside Europe. In Sweden, which has the largest immigrant population, it is presently estimated that approximately one-tenth of its inhabitants are foreign-born or the children of foreign-born parents—a proportion not far below that of the United States during its heaviest periods of immigration. The experience of their earlier countrymen in America is thus proving valuable to present-day Scandinavians in dealing with their own new world.

H. Arnold Barton
Professor emeritus
Southern Illinois University

Icelanders on board Camoens, one of the best known ships bringing emigrants from Iceland, probably in 1887.
Photo Sigfús Eymundsson. © The National Museum of Iceland.

Celebration of the 4th of July in Rebild,
Denmark. Photo Kirkegård.

A winter portrait around 1912 of Ketill Valgarðsson and Soffía Sveinbjörnsdóttir. Their grandson is Bill Valgardsson, one of the foremost contemporary writers in Canada. © Manitoba Archives.

It was common for emigrants to have their picture taken upon the arrival at Ellis Island and so did this Finnish family. © Ellis Island Museum.

The Norwegian immigrant Mina Westbye "on her own claim" in Minnesota around 1904. Mina Westbye in white bonnet. She called her claim "Trysil". © Norsk Utvandrermuseum.

Ingeborg Folkedahl Johnsen and the neighbor's son, Iver Bang, in Lands, North Dakota in 1902. © Norwegian-American Historical Association.

Men from Hallingdal and Numedal in Norway working as loggers in Whatcom county, Washington 1903. In front of the log, from the left: Svein Mykstui, Svein Garnaas, Knut Bogstrand, Ole Grøtjorden, Kittil Mykstui, Ole Harang. On top of the log, from the left: Even Jellum, Erik Garnaas, Knut Jellum. © Norsemen's Federation.

Danish paint shop in Chicago.

Train at station in Vining, Otter Tail Co., Minnesota. © Norsk Utvandrermuseum.

Norse Hotel, Decorah, Iowa, around 1910. © Vesterheim Norwegian-American Museum.

Victor Borge reading a fairy tale at the unveiling of the H.C. Andersen statue in Central Park, New York in 1956.

An Icelandic farmer in Manitoba, called Litli-Mundi, holding his sheep. Many of the Icelanders tried to continue with the old way of farming from back home, such as the rearing of sheep even though Manitoba did not offer similar grazing grounds as the Icelandic mountains.
© Manitoba Archives.

Icelandic pioneer woman spinning in 1905. Women kept up their traditional work around the house. Many of them had a chance to make a living on their own in the towns and cities by getting employed as house maids.
© Manitoba Archives.

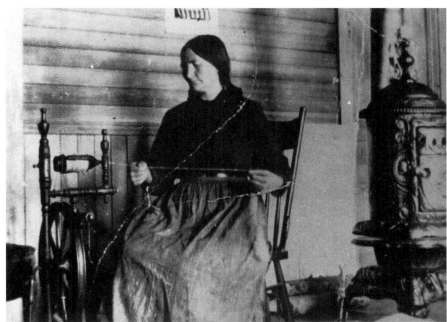

Family of Kristin K. Rensla, outside Towner, Mc Henry Co., North Dakota.
© Norsk Utvandrermuseum.

Transporting fish on Lake Winnipeg. The fish in the lake was one of the reasons why the Icelanders regarded new Ice-
land in Manitoba as an ideal location for their settlement. They were good fishermen from back home, but the ice on
the lake was new to them and they had to develop an entirely new technique in order to fish through the ice.
© Manitoba Archives.

The village of Vopnafjörður in 1881, one of the largest ports for emigrants from Iceland.
The ship furthest out is to pick up emigrants. Photo Sigfús Eymundsson.
© The National museum of Iceland.

The journey to the port of Hanko in Finland was long and the emigrants often had to wait several days for their ship at the emigrant hotel. © Hanko Museum.

A Danish bookstore in Texas. © The Danish Emigration Archives.

Mrs. Beret Hagebak outside her sod house in Lac Que Parle County, Minnesota around 1870. The claim was known as "The Skinnbrokstedet" (Leather Pants Place). Travellers stopped here to water their horses and drink a cup of coffee. "With our hearts and minds." © Minnesota Historical society.

Helmi and Klaus Ruotsalainen's first home in Rock, Michigan 1914. © The Institute of Migration.

People from Saelebote, Veggli, in Setesdal, Norway, leaving for America 1895.
The neighbors have come to bid them farewell.
© S. Aarvelta, Veggli.

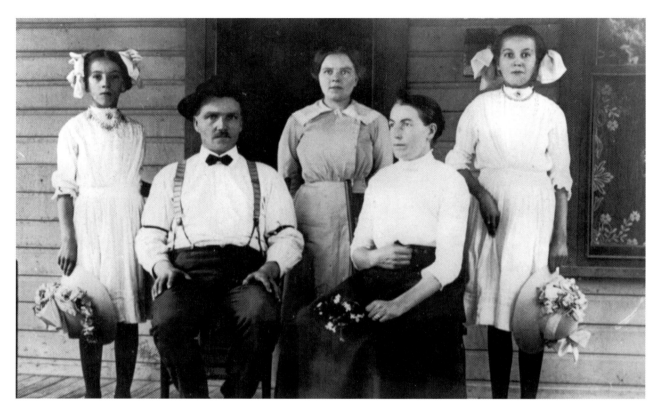

Anna and Oskar Snickars from Närpes, Finland moved to San Francisco shortly after the turn of the century and sent this picture back home with the text: "Greetings from Anna and Oskar and the girls to Grandmother".
© The Institute of Migration.

Leaving Seljestad Stage Station, Røldal, Norway, ca. 1900. Photograph Axel Lindahl.
© Norsk Folkemuseum, Anders B. Wilse Collections.

Charles Samuelson in front of his grocery store in Seven Corners, Minneapolis. The store was founded around 1887.
© The Swedish Emigrant Institute.

A tailor shop in Chicago's Swede town. Swedes often worked as tailors and seamstresses in America.
© The Swedish Emigrant Institute.

Threshing scene at Alfred's. 1909.
© The Swedish Emigrant Institute.

Scene from Swede Town in Chicago. The little girl on the picture is Selma Jacobson.
In the 1880's the Swedes were so numerous that Chicago Avenue was called
"The Swedish Snoose Boulevard".
© The Swedish Emigrant Institute.

An Icelandic farm, Haugakil in Borgafjörður around 1890 built in a traditional manner of stone and turf. The women's headdress became a laughing stock in America and was considered symbolic for the old way of thinking back "home". Photo Sigfús Eymundsson.
© The National Museum of Iceland.

Finnish miners in Red Lodge around 1904. Persons identified are Matti Saari from Veteli, Kalle Aalto from Kiikka, Herman Jansson and Emil Känsälä from Kaustinen.
© The Institute of Migration.

The Danish old people's home. San Rafael, California.
©The Danish Emigration Archives.

Suggested further reading

Åberg, Alf. *The People of New Sweden.* Stockholm: Natur och Kultur, 1987.

Barton, H. Arnold. *A Folk Divided: Homeland Swedes and Swedish Americans, 1840-1940.* Carbondale, IL: Southern Illinois Univ. Press, 1994.

Hoglund, A. William. *Finnish Immigrants in America, 1880-1920.* Madison, WI: Univ. of Wisconsin Press, 1960.

Jordan, Terry & Matti Kaups, *The American Backwoods Frontier: An Ethnic and Ecological Interpretation.* Baltimore: Johns Hopkins Univ. Press, 1989.

Kero, Reino. The Finns in North America: Destinations and Composition of Immigrant Societies in North America before World War I. Turku. Turun Yliopisto B 150, 190.

–. Migration from Finland to North America in the Years between the United States Civil War and the First World War. Turku: Institute of Migration Studies CI, 1974.

Ljungmark, Lars. *Swedish Exodus.* Carbondale, IL: Southern Illinois Univ. Press, 1973; reprinted with updated bibliography, 1996.

Lovoll, Odd S. *The Promise of America: A History of the Norwegian-American People.* Minneapolis: Univ. of Minnesota Press, 1984.

–. *The Promise Fulfilled: A Portrait of Norwegian Americans Today.* Minneapolis: Univ. of Minnesota Press, 1998.

Nelson, Helge. *The Swedes and the Swedish Settlements in North America,* 2 vols. Lund: Skrifter utgivna av Kungl. Humanistiska vetenskapssamfundet i Lund, 1943.

Nielsen, George R. *The Danish Americans.* Boston: Twayne Publishers, 1981.

Niitemaa, Vilho et. al (eds.). Old Friends – Strong Ties. Turku. Institute of Migration, 1976.

Norman, Hans. *Transatlantic Connections: Nordic Migration to the New World after 1800.* Oslo: Norwegian University Press, 1988.

Qualey, Carlton C. *Norwegian Settlement in the United States.* Northfield, MN: Norwegian-American Historical Association, 1938.

Runblom, Harald & Hans Norman, eds. *From Sweden to America: A History of the Migrtation.* Minneapolis: Univ. of Minnesota Press, 1976.

Semmingsen, Ingrid. *From Norway to America: A History of the Migration.* Minneapolis: Univ. of Minnesota Press, 1978.

The principal periodicals on Nordic emigration and Nordic-American history are *Norwegian-American Studies,* published since 1926 by the Norwegian-American Historical Association; the *Swedish-American Historical Quarterly,* published since 1950 by the Swedish-American Historical Society; *The Bridge,* published since 1977 by the Danish-American Heritage Society; *The Bridge,* published by the Emigrant Register in Karlstad Sweden; and the *Swedish American Genealogist,* since 1980, now published by the Swenson Swedish Immigration Research Center.

The website **http:// www.migrationinstitute.fi/nordic** gives access to free searchable Nordic emigrant databases and provides general information on the great overseas emigration and links to websites on Nordic genealogy.

Links and addresses to American-Scandinavian organizations and institutions are also provided.

Addresses

Det Danske Udvandrerarkiv
The Danish Emigration Archives
Arkivstræde 1
P.O. Box 1731
DK - 9100 Aalborg, Denmark
phone: +45 99 31 42 20
fax: +45 98 10 22 48
bfl-kultur@aalborg.dk
http://users.cybercity.dk/~ccc13656/home.htm

Samfundet for dansk genealogi & personalhistorie
The Society for Danish Genealogy and Biography
Finn Andersen
Grysgårdsvej 2
DK-2400 København NV, Denmark
info@genealogi.dk
http://www.genealogi.dk/index_us.htm

Siirtolaisuusinstituutti
Migrationsinstitutet
Institute of Migration
Piispankatu 3
FIN – 20500 Turku, Finland
phone: +358 22317536
fax: +358 22333460
joukork@utu.fi
http://www.migrationinstitute.fi

Vörå Emigrationscenter Finland
PB 20
FIN-66600 VÖRÅ, Finland
phone: +358 6 383 2117
fax: +358 6 382 0255
emicenter@vora.fi
http://www.vora.fi/emicenter/

Ålands Emigrantinstitut
The Åland Islands' Emigrant Institute
Ålandsvägen 48
FIN-22 100 Mariehamn, Åland
phone: +358 18 13 325
emi.inst@aland.net

The Genealogical Society of Finland
Liisankatu 16 A
FIN-00170 Helsinki, Finland
phone: +358-9-278 1188
fax: +358-9-278 1199
seura@genealogia.fi
http://www.genealogia.fi

Vesturfarasetrið
The Icelandic Emigration Center
565 Hofsós, Iceland
phone: +354 453 7935
fax: +354 453 7936
vestur@krokur.is
http://www.krokur.is/~vestur/english/index.html

Stofnun Árna Magnussonar á Íslandi
The Árni Magnússon Institute in Iceland
Sudurgötu
IS – 101 Reykjavik, Iceland
phone: + 354- 525 4010
fax: + 354- 525 4035
http://am.hi.is/

Ættfræðifélagið
The Icelandic Genealogy Society
Ármúla 19
108 - Reykjavík
Iceland
phone: +354-588-2450
aett@vortex.is
http://www.vortex.is/aett

Norsk Utvandrermuseum
The Norwegian Emigrant Museum
Åkershagan
N-2312 Ottestad, Norway
phone: +47 62 57 48 50
fax: +47 62 57 48 51
museum@emigrant.museum.no
http://www.hamarnett.no/emigrantmuseum/

Det Norske Utvandrersenteret
The Norwegian Emigration Center
Strandkaien 31
N-4005 Stavanger, Norway
phone: +47 5153 8860
fax: +47 5153 8863
detnu@online.no
http://www.emigrationcenter.com/index.htm

Norsk Slektshistorisk Forening
The Norwegian Genealogical Association
Postboks 59 Sentrum
N-0101 Oslo, Norway
nstgen@online.no
http://home.sol.no/~nstgen/engdx.htm

Svenska Emigrantinstitutet
Swedish Emigrant Institute
Vilhelm Mobergs gata 4
Box 201
S-351 04 Växjö, Sweden
phone: +46 470-20120
fax: +46 470-39416
info@svenskaemigrantinstitutet.g.se
http://www.svenskaemigrantinstitutet.g.se/eng.html

Emigrantregistret
Kinship Center
Box 331
Hööksgatan 2
S-651 08 Karlstad, Sweden
phone: +46 54 107726
fax: +46 54 107701
research@emigrantregistret.s.se
http://www.emigrantregistret.s.se/

Riksföreningen Sverigekontakt
Box 53066
S-40014 Göteborg, Sweden

phone: + 46- 31 180062
fax: + 46 –31 209902
sverigekontakt@tripnet.se
http://www.sverigekontakt.o.se/

Migranternas hus
House of Migrants
Ungmansvägen 3
S-822 30 Alfta, Sweden
phone: +46 271 10861
fax: +46 271 55726
alfta@migranternas-hus.x.se
http://www.migranternas-hus.x.se/english/index.htm

Sveriges Släktforskarförbund
Federation of Swedish Genealogical Societies
Håkan Skogsjö
Tordmulegränd 6
FIN-22100 Mariehamn, Finland
phone: +358-1821204
hskogsjo@aland.net
http://www.genealogi.se/index.htm

Addresses to Scandinavian-North American Organizations in the field of migration and genealogy

Danish

The Danish Immigrant Museum
2212 Washington Street,
P O Box 470
Elk Horn, Iowa 51531-0470
phone: 712-764-7001, 800-759-9192
fax: 712-764-7002
dkmus@netins.net
http://dkmuseum.org/

Danish Immigrant Archives
Grandview College
1351 Grandview Avenue
Des Moines, Iowa 50316

Dana College
Blair, Nebraska 68008-1099
http://www.dana.edu/

Danish American Heritage Society
4105 Stone Brooke Road
Ames, Iowa 50010

Federations of Danish Associations in Canada
679 Eastvale Court
Gloucester, Ontario K1J 6Z7

Finnish

The Finnish-American Heritage Center
601 Quincy
Hancock, Michigan 49930
phone: (906) 487-7367
fax: (906) 487-7366
http://www.suomi.edu

Swedish Finn Historical Society
P.O. Box 17264
Seattle, WA 98107-0964
phone: 206-706-0738
fax: 206-782-5813
sfhs@gte.net
http://home1.gte.net/SFHS/index.htm

The Finnish Center at Saima Park, Inc.
P.O. Box 30
Fitchburg, MA 01420

Canadian Friends of Finland
Secretary Varpu Lindström
PO 206, Stn A
Willowdale, Ontario, M2N 5S8
phone: 416-730-8350
varpul@yorku.ca

Vancouver Finlandia Club
6540 Thomas St.
Burnaby, BC, V5B 4B9
phone: 604-294-2777
fax: 604-294-5932
http://www3.bc.sympatico.ca/finlandiaclub/

Icelandic

New Iceland Heritage Museum
c/o Tammy Axelsson
Box 235
Gimli, MB, R0C 1B0, CANADA
phone: 204 642 4001
fax: 204 642 7151
safn@mb.sympatico.ca

Nelson Gerrard, historian
Box 925
Arborg, Manitoba, R0C 0A0, CANADA
phone: 204 378 2758

The Stephan G. Stephansson House
c/o Bernice Andersen, President
Box 837
Markerville, AB T0M 1M04, CANADA
phone: 403 728 3595
fax: 403 728 3225
Creamery@touralberta.com
http://www.gov.ab.ca/mcd/mhs/steph/steph.htm

Icelandic National League of North America
Box 99
Gimli, MB., R0C 1B0, CANADA
inl@ecn.mb.ca
http://users.imag.net/~sry.rasgeirs/INL-Chapters.html

Norwegian

Sons of Norway
1455 W. Lake Street
Minneapolis, MN 55408
phone: 612 827 3611
fax: 612 827 0658
http://www.sofn.com

Bygdelagenes Fellesraad
v/ Marilyn Somdahl
10129 Goodrich Circle
Minneapolis, MN 55437
phone: 612 831 4409

Norwegian-American Historical Association
St. Olaf College
1510 St. Olaf Avenue
Northfield, MN 55057-1097
phone: (507) 646 3221
naha@stolaf.edu
http://www.naha.stolaf.edu

Vesterheim
Norwegian-American Museum
523 W. Water Street
P.O. Box 379
Decorah, IA 52101
phone: (319) 382-9681
vesterheim@vesterheim.org
www.vesterheim.org

Nordic Heritage Museum
3014 NW 67th Street
Seattle, WA 98117
phone: (206) 789-5707
nordic@intelistep.com
www.nordicmuseum.com

Sweden

Swedish-American Historical Society
North Park University
5125 N. Spaulding Avenue
Chicago, IL 60625
phone: (773) 583-5722
kanders@northpark.edu

Swenson Swedish Immigration Research Center
Augustana College
639 38th Street
Rock Island, Il 61201
phone: (309) 794-7221
sag@augustana.edu
www.augustana.edu/administration/swenson

American-Swedish Historical Museum
1900 Pattison Avenue
Philadelphia, PA 19145
phone: (215) 389-1776
ashm@libertynet.org
www.libertynet.org

American-Swedish Institute
2600 Park Avenue
Minneapolis, MN 55407
phone: (612) 871 4907
information@americanswedishinst.org
www.americanswedishinst.org

Swedish Council of America
2600 Park Avenue
Minneapolis, MN 55407
phone: (612) 871 0593
www.swedishcouncil.org

Swedish-American Museum Center of Chicago
5211 N. Clark Street
Chicago, IL 60640
phone: (773) 728- 8111
Museum@samac.org
www.samac.org